What Women Want*

By Jennifer Siegel

Illustrations by Carlos Marrero

* What Men Need to Know

BRIGHT SKY PRESS

Albany, Texas · New York, New York

10 9 8 7 6 5 4 3 2 1

Book and cover design by Kathryn Plosica/Two Rivers Design

ISBN 1-931721-03-3

Printed in China through Asia Pacific Offset

Dedication

I thought about dedicating this book to my children (my greatest gifts) or to my husband (my greatest gift giver) but then I thought better of it.

   I hereby dedicate this book to my girlfriends, and to girlfriends everywhere. Women who have faked joyful smiles at bad gifts for years. Women who have pretended to LOVE that green sweater when they hinted for three months to get diamond studs. Women who spent Valentine's Day euphoric in anticipation, and Valentine's Night clutching a 7-11 rose. And to the men who love them, but whose gifts don't reflect that love one bit! Carry this book with you everywhere...PLEASE!

Introduction

A few years ago I had a huge disappointment in my life. I bought a house with my dad, a semi-retired builder, to renovate and resell as an investment. This was a dream come true for me, to work with my dad, create something beautiful that we could both be proud of, and make a small fortune. I got the first two, but when it came down to the selling part, it didn't go as planned. With my heart damaged, and my spirit broken, I couldn't seem to get over the feeling-sorry-for-myself syndrome.

After work on a Friday afternoon, my husband, Mo, came home a little earlier than usual, and was accompanied by my cousin Susan. I was then informed that Susan was staying with the children and I was leaving with my husband. So I did. In the back seat was an overnight bag (he even remembered my toothbrush) and a small box of wrapped gifts. We took off into the mountains, with a night of surprises and cheering up on Mo's agenda. All of my questions regarding the night's plan went unanswered, and I realized that I needed to go with the flow and enjoy, so I did.

First stop: a view of Longs Peak, a majestic 14,000 foot mountain that he knew would make me cry as great settings always do, and then my first gift—a small brass hammer with a note that said:

The beauty that you create will come back to you.

Then, off to a romantic inn, nestled on a country road, outside Rocky Mountain National Park. We walked up creaky stairs to our room, complete with a claw foot bathtub—tears again—followed by gift number two: bubble bath and another note: A little something to help you soak away your sadness. So I did. Dinner at this enchanted inn was just what anyone could hope for—rustic and yummy, complete with a piano player who reminded me of Buffalo Bill. After a long and loving dinner spent gazing and hand holding, Mo gave me my final gift: A paper cut-out badge of courage signed by Mo and our children, with a note saying: It takes a brave woman to make dreams come true. So I will.

I know how important gifts are in a person's life, and I know what women want...

A convertible
dated the year
she was born.

Custody of the clicker

for a week.

WARNING
Do not do this during
football season.
You will grow to hate her.

9

A bucket
of daisies.

A rose bush...planted.

Surprise her, almost any
surprise will do.

A journal
because her
thoughts
should be written down.

Her birthstone.

Pearls.

A pearl.

13

A

bubble bath waiting with

wine, candles, etc...

don't get in,

this one's for her alone.

15

Listen for thirty minutes
without interrupting.

A whistle. In case she ever
needs you just...

Jay's hikes into the mountains provide precious solitude for him. Several times a week he heads to the hills for exercise and contemplation, but still he takes Catherine with him. She knows this, because of the small gifts he offers her upon his return. Sometimes it's a perfect pine cone, or a deer antler for her collection.

17

Give her a foot massage and pedicure.

Write her a
message in rose petals.

A fancy tissue box holder
(if she's a wet one).

A written list
of the reasons
that you love her.

Thirty gifts for her
30th birthday—
all individually wrapped.

A down comforter
and a good book.

23

Diamond stud earrings presented in a non-traditional way.

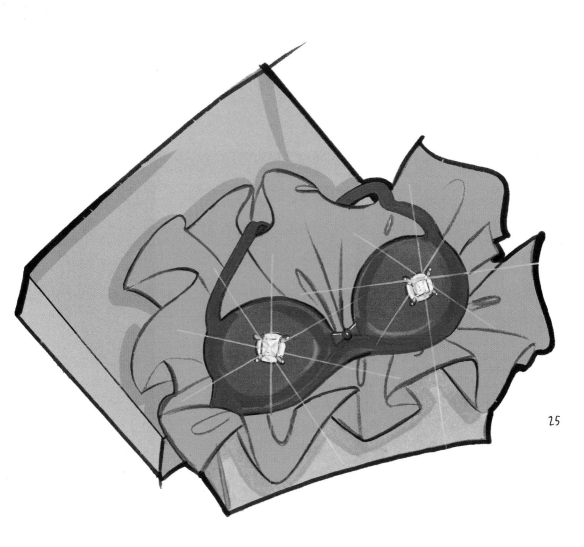

25

A musical instrument she played in her childhood.

An old-fashioned love letter mailed to her house even, or especially, if you live there too.

Angela planned a dinner party for the family with whom she lived while an exchange student in Italy. She had encouraged this family to visit for years and they finally accepted her invitation. Angela fretted over the preparations, wanting everything to be just right. On the eve of their visit, her husband Tony announced that he had taken the next day off to cook a special meal, a traditional Italian feast.

Thanks to Tony's gift, Angela's reunion was perfect.

Compliment
her mother for raising
such a great daughter.

29

Make a donation
to the charity that
touches her heart.

Give her a case of the

wine that she enjoyed
at dinner last week.

Kay always dreamed of going to the Rocky Mountains, but when Jack became ill, their dream of hiking through Colorado became unattainable. For their fortieth anniversary, Jack presented her with a painting of Pike's Peak and a note that said, "Since we cannot come to the mountain, the mountain will come to you."

A gift certificate
for five more minutes,
redeemable
anytime.

A framed photograph of her pet.

Tell her 5 good things about herself for every criticism, forever.

By the time Maureen was about to turn fifty, she was living in an empty nest.

With all of her children gone, she looked back on her life and wondered what kind of an impact she had really made. During this difficult time, she also wondered why Bill had chosen to miss their bridge night two weeks in a row. At her fiftieth birthday dinner, all five children presented her with a list of fifty reasons they loved her so much, a project her husband had secretly orchestrated during his nights away.

Do her home jobs
for a week.

An indoor picnic
on a snowy night
complete with
plastic ants.

39

Go shopping with her
and be a good sport.

41

A framed picture of her and her dad.

After Pam became single again she ran into an old friend who soon became her new flame. During all her years of married life, Pam never received a meaningful Christmas gift, but her first Christmas with Kenny was filled with thought-fulness — simply the best holiday she ever had. Kenny bought a pair of her favorite jeans (he looked in the closet, checked the size and got it right!), a cordless drill because she once mentioned it would come in handy, and snow boots because he remembered that her feet got wet when they went sledding the month before — and he wrapped them all himself.

Tell her you love her
at least 5 times a day,
especially when she
doesn't deserve it.

A gift certificate
for one
GIRLS NIGHT OUT
per month till
her next birthday.

A framed postcard
of the city or town where
she was born.

If she's from the beach,
have someone send you sand.

If she's from the East,
have someone send
you leaves
in the fall.

Your three favorite books
inscribed to her.

Put every
pillow in the house,
your comforter, and
a bottle of wine
in front of
a roaring fire.

51

A gift box
that contains both
flannel pajamas and a
sexy teddy with a note
that says "I love you
no matter how
you are wrapped."

53

Bring her
cookies and milk
in bed.

54

A trip to her hometown.

Marie and her husband Paul planned a walking trip through Ireland for her thirtieth birthday. This was a mixed blessing for Marie, because she had three small boys at home whom she had never left. All through the planning process, Marie was worried about leaving the boys even though her sister would be taking care of them. Upon their arrival at JFK, they were met by Marie's three best girlfriends from college. In shock, she turned to Paul; and asked, "Are they all going?" "Yes," he said with a smile, "and I'm staying home with the boys".

A
beach vacation

in february,

or...

57

Piña coladas,
a Hawaiian shirt, and the
sounds of Jimmy Buffett
in february.

59

Take her and her
girlfriends out to dinner.

Rent her favorite movie,
watch it with her,
and supply the snacks.

*P*lant a tulip for every year
you have loved her.

When Joanne's mother was diagnosed with terminal cancer, Joanne was devastated. Her husband Jim looked beyond the years of mother-in-law torment and sold his Harley Davidson motorcycle for cash. He presented Joanne's mom and dad with tickets to Hawaii, a place they had always wanted to go. After dropping off Joanne's parents at the airport, Jim played a tape of Don Ho's greatest hits, and they laughed and cried all the way home.

*B*ring her morning coffee.

Compliment her cooking,
no matter what.

A football jersey
from your favorite team
and an invitation to
watch with the boys.

Call the Chamber
of Commerce in
her hometown and have
the local newspaper
sent on her birthday.

The sheet music to her favorite song.

A copy of her favorite children's book (ask her mom).

Tell her she's beautiful when she believes it least and needs to hear it most.

Buy her a piece of jewelry for the birth of every child. Diamonds are good.

71

Do you have a pickup truck? (you may want to get one).

Put a mattress in the back with beautiful bedding (that means clean matching sheets and pillows) a bottle of wine, good glasses (that means no plastic), romantic music and a remote stargazing spot.

6 piano lessons,

6 ballet classes, etc...

Make a childhood dream

come alive again.

Start and warm up her car
in the morning.

Surprise her with a day
off from work, a hotel key,
and room service.

Did I mention diamonds?

How many times in the course of a year do you see something that is "just perfect" for someone else and you don't buy it because either it's not their birthday, or the holidays aren't for a few months. It's not that you can't afford it or that the person doesn't deserve it but for some reason you just don't do it.

How many times in the course of a year do you see something good or even wonderful in another person and you don't acknowledge it. You see it, it's as plain as day, but for some reason—maybe you're too shy, or too busy—you stop just short of telling them. Just short of making them smile.

And finally, how many times do you feel love in your heart without expressing it.

Charlene's Story

My friend Charlene died last winter. She fought with cancer for as long as she could until it won. My last memory of her was two days before she died, sitting up in her hospital bed, surrounded by friends and family. Beautiful. Confident. Defying her thin frame and bald head by wearing a tiara. The gift of her humor still intact to make everyone feel more at ease.

Nine months before Charlene was diagnosed, she completed the construction of her dream home. From my bedroom window I saw this house go up in record time, from a foundation to a castle in less than a year, all under her watchful eye. Standing in the snow and rain, with her hands on her hips, from dawn till dusk, both bossing and charming every builder, plumber and craftsman, she willed her house up as fast as she could—an urgent gift of a home for her family. Not knowing, but perhaps sensing, her time was short.

Charlene had only nine months in her new home before the news of her condition came, and when it did she both fought for her life and planned for her death. She loved flowers—her gardens were important to her—so she planted hundreds of tulips, a constant springtime reminder and gift.

And then there was the dinner—another gift to her friends. After her funeral service Charlene wanted her friends to have her dream party, even if she couldn't be there. So she planned the dinner, down to the white china plates. Here are some of her instructions: "All of those great wines in the cellar we've been saving for the right moment? Open them and pour them in the Waterford glasses with abandon and joy. I want prime rib...no poached salmon...no I want you to have both! And truffles, dozens of chocolate truffles. Don't you dare leave a single flower in the church; fill the house to the brim with my beloved flowers."

With every detail discussed, every desire expressed, she could go on to a better place. Thank you Charlene. Knowing you was a gift.